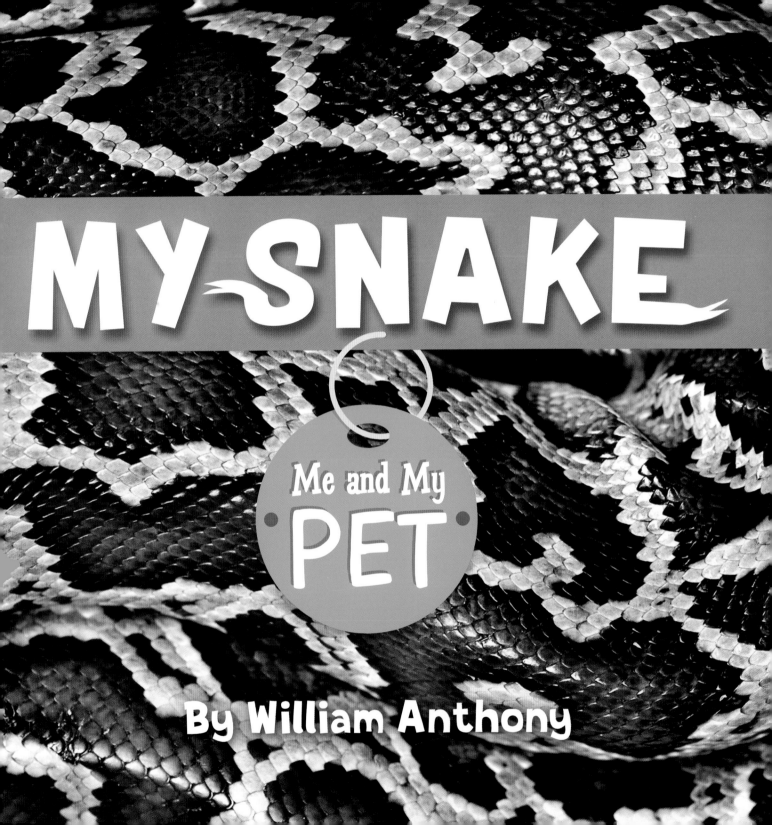

MY SNAKE

Me and My
PET

By William Anthony

BookLife
PUBLISHING

©2019
BookLife Publishing Ltd.
King's Lynn
Norfolk PE30 4LS

A catalogue record for this
book is available from the
British Library.

ISBN: 978-1-78637-576-6

Written by:
William Anthony

Edited by:
Madeline Tyler

Designed by:
Jasmine Pointer

Photocredits:
Images are courtesy of Shutterstock.com. With thanks to Getty Images, Thinkstock Photo and iStockphoto.

Front cover - Duplass, dangdumrong. 2 - Krisda Ponchaipulltawee. 3 - Eric Isselee, Kuznetsov Alexey. 4 - Duplass. 5 - Lana Langlois. 6 - BIGANDT.COM. 7 - VinceBradley. 8 - Sergey Novikov. 9 - halimqd. 10 - SasinTipchai. 11 - Duplass. 12 - Marek Velechovsky. 13 - Skynavin. 14 - Supershine. 15 - pattyphotoart. 16 - pixinoo. 17 - Eric Isselee. 18 - getideaka. 19 - Mark_Kostich. 20 - Tom Grundy. 21 - Somporn Pramong. 22 - Africa Studio. 23 - Sergey Novikov.

CONTENTS

Words that look like this can be found in the glossary on page 24.

Jay and Monty

Hello! My name's Jay, and this is my pet snake, Monty. He's twelve years old. Snakes are my favourite animal because they have cool patterns on them!

Jay →

Whether you're thinking about getting one, or you've had one for a little while, Monty and I are going to take you through how to look after a snake.

Lead the way, Monty!

Monty

Getting a Snake

Looking after a snake means you are going to have a lot of <u>responsibility</u>. You will need to feed them, and give them a nice home with lots of places to hide.

My family got Monty from a pet shop but you can get snakes from other places too. You can also get a snake from a breeder. This is someone who keeps snakes to **mate** them.

Always make sure you **research** the person or place you're buying a pet from.

Home

The glass stops your snake from escaping.

Snakes need a very special type of home. Your snake will need to be kept in a vivarium (say: viv-air-ee-um). A vivarium is like a house for your snake, but it has glass walls.

A vivarium also keeps things nice and warm for your snake. Snakes are **cold-blooded**, so your vivarium will need to be warm at one end and cool at the other.

Viper Snake in the Wild

Playtime

Different types of snakes like doing different things.
Leave lots of branches and rocks in their vivarium
so they have things to climb!

Monty likes coming out to play with us. All snakes are different, so don't force your snake to play with you if they don't want to. Always be calm and gentle with your snake.

My dad and my sister like to pet Monty, too!

Food

Feeding time is the least fun part of looking after a snake. A snake's **diet** is usually made up of dead mice or rats. Your snake will need to be fed once a week.

When your snake knows that food is coming, they can get very excited. They might even think your hand is food by accident. It is a good idea to get an adult to feed your snake.

Snakes can be dangerous pets.

Bedtime

Snakes are not like us when they sleep. We sleep at night after a long day, but snakes can sleep at any time – this could be at night or during the day.

Snakes don't have eyelids, so they still look awake when they're asleep!

You could put a little cave or a pile of bark in your snake's vivarium. This is a nice, dark place for your snake to take a little nap.

The Vet

Vets are like doctors, but for animals instead of humans!

Snakes can get ill, just like humans. Snakes that are ill can go to the vets. The vet will do everything they can to help your snake get better again.

If you think your snake isn't very well, make sure you tell someone.

One day when I came home, Monty was breathing loudly from his mouth. Snakes should breathe from their nostrils. I told my parents and we took him to the vets, who made him all better again!

17

Growing Up

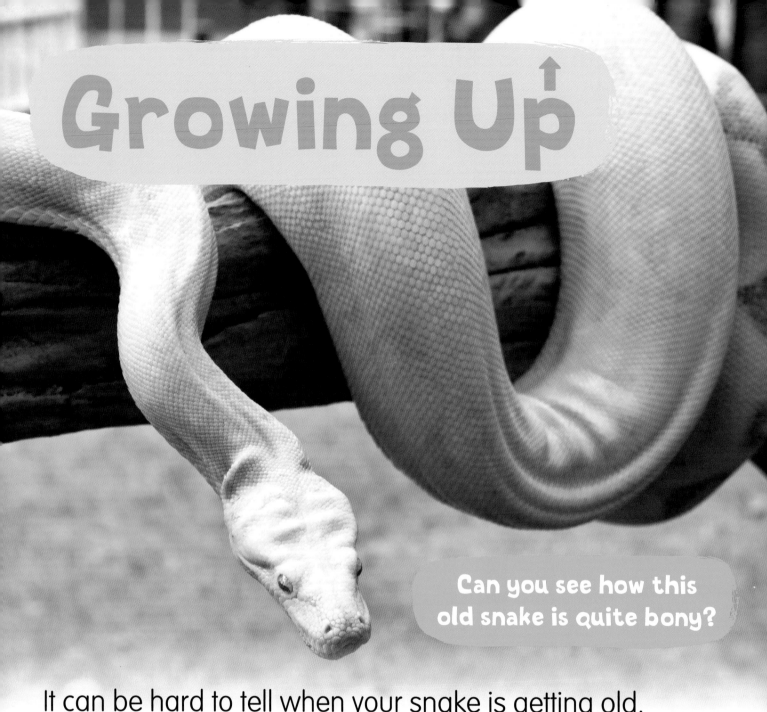

Can you see how this old snake is quite bony?

It can be hard to tell when your snake is getting old. Sometimes old snakes will get a bit bonier, or they might need longer breaks between feeds.

As your snake grows up, you might notice them start to shed their skin. All animals lose old, dead skin, but most do so slowly. Snakes lose their old skin all in one go!

Super Snakes

All pet snakes are amazing, but some wild snakes are simply super! There is a type of snake in Asia with a very special trick…

...it can fly! The flying snake jumps from tree to tree by moving its body in an 'S' shape. Don't expect your snake to be able to fly though – flying snakes have <u>adapted</u> to do this.

You ♥ and Your Pet

Whether you've got your new snake or you're about to get one, make sure you take care of them just like Monty and I have taught you!

I'm sure you'll make a great pet owner. Try to think of what your snake would like in the wild and make their vivarium like that. Most of all, make sure you enjoy your new scaly friend!

GLOSSARY

adapted	changed over time to suit the environment
cold-blooded	animals whose blood changes with the temperature around them
diet	the kinds of food that an animal or person usually eats
mate	to produce young with an animal of the same species
research	the activity of getting information about a subject
responsibility	having tasks that you are expected to do

INDEX